MEET EDWARD

Written by Tracy Voss

Illustrated by Marcy Tippmann

Dedication

This book, the first in the **Live Like a Dog PAWS** program, is dedicated to my five-year-old self. This program is everything I wish I had been taught about animals when I was a child. I truly believe I would have started this mission earlier and my childhood dog Bear would have received better care than she did. At the time, I didn't know any better. The unconditional love of Bear and all my dogs after her has taught me about forgiveness and living in the moment. The secret to happiness is to Live Like a Dog.

Meet Edward—The Real-Life Ambassador for PAWS
©2022 Tracy Voss
All rights reserved.
Except for brief excerpts for review purposes, no part of this book may be reproduced or used in any form without written permission from the publisher. For more information about this book or the author, visit LiveLikeaDog.press.

ISBN 978-1-7377470-4-8 - *Meet Edward,* paperback
ISBN 978-1-7377470-6-2 - *Meet Edward,* Spanish translation
eISBN 978-1-7377470-5-5 - *Meet Edward* ebook

First edition 2022
Printed in the United States of America
Live Like a Dog, LLC
PO Box 849
Hondo, TX 78861
LiveLikeaDog.press

Book Designer: Marcy Tippmann
Project Manager: Andrea Leigh Ptak

Hi! Welcome to the Live Like a Dog PAWS program. I am so excited you are here!

My name is Edward.

I used to be a stray dog living on the streets of Brownsville, Texas. I had no one to take care of me. I was hungry, full of bugs, and when it rained I got really wet. I didn't even have a bed to sleep on at night or blankets to keep me warm when it was cold.

My only friends were the kids who played with me on their way to school. Sometimes, they fed me their lunch so I wouldn't be hungry. They liked to give me scratches on my back because I was always itchy.

Edward Says...

If you see a stray dog, always make sure to get an adult to help. Not all dogs are nice like me. Some are so scared that they could bite.

I'm a pretty cool dog, but I know that I am different, too.

Sometimes, kids stare at my toes because they have never seen toes like mine before.

Would you like to see my toes?

They have looked this way since I was born. I limp a little bit when I walk, but that doesn't stop me from running around and having fun.

My teeth are also unusual because they are brown instead of white.

Would you like to see my teeth?

My teeth are like this because I had a fever when I was a puppy. The fever was so high, it turned my teeth brown. The color of my teeth doesn't bother me, though. I still enjoy food and treats!

I may be different, but I am a good dog. And guess what? Kids love me just the way I am. They love me as much as I love them.

That's what is so awesome about dogs. Dogs love you even when your hair sticks up all weird or when your breath smells like rotten eggs.

We never make fun of you if you make a mistake or if you are different. We love you just the way you are.

After living on the streets for a few years, my life completely changed one day. An animal control officer picked me up and took me to the animal shelter.

The animal shelter was really crowded with dogs and cats. My ears hurt from all of the dogs barking at the same time.

There was another dog named Teddy in the same cage as me. He told me that he had lived his whole life chained to a tree in the backyard.

Tracy is part of an animal rescue group that helps dogs like us who don't have homes of our own. We stay at Oliver's House until we are adopted by nice families.

Now, we sleep inside on nice, soft beds and always have plenty of food. Tracy and her helpers take really good care of us.

I started to feel sad, though. After months and months of waiting, no one wanted to adopt me. All of the other dogs left for their new homes—everyone but me.

I wondered why no one would choose me.
Was it because of my toes and my brown teeth?
There had to be a place for me, too.

One day, I asked Tracy, "Why doesn't anyone want to adopt me?"

She gave me a big hug and said, "Sometimes special dogs like you have a special purpose."

Then, Tracy decided to choose me for a special project called PAWS!

PAWS stands for **P**romoting **A**nimal **W**elfare in **S**chools.

Tracy knew that I would be perfect for this project. Now, I get to go to schools in Texas to teach kids like you about helping animals!

Edward Says...

All kids can help dogs, no matter where you live. You can help the dogs that live with you, or dogs in your area that don't have a home. PAWS will show you how!

e Ff Gg Hh Ii Jj Kk Ll Mm Nn Oo Pp Qq Rr Ss Tt Uu Vv Ww
PAWS
Program
Tracy and
Edward

I know that might sound funny, but dogs are almost always happy, and we can teach you so many things about being happy, too.

I'll bet you never knew you could learn something from a dog, but you can!

I have books to share with you about real rescue dogs like me, fun activities to teach you about helping animals, and a whole lot more. I am so happy that you are a part of the PAWS program with me.

Always remember to Live Like a Dog!

PAWS, Promoting Animal Welfare in Schools

PAWS is an educational program for elementary school children that encourages compassion for all living creatures.

Live Like A Dog PAWS teaches children through educational books and hands-on learning activities how to become ambassadors for responsible pet ownership and kindness to all living creatures—including people.

Live Like A Dog PAWS develops and strengthens the human-animal bond which can be a source of comfort for many children who have difficulties at home or at school.

All young children need support and guidance to have healthy relationships within their immediate families and friends. This includes relationships with their pets. For many kids, their pets are their best friends. For some children, their pets might provide the only stable relationship and unconditional love they experience while they are growing up.

Strengthening the human-animal bond can improve self-esteem and give children a sense of purpose as well as encouraging them to show compassion towards all living creatures. This program will provide children with helpful tools that they can use to lead happy lives, despite the many challenges they may face in their life.

It is our belief that every child desires to provide their pets with the same quality of care they deserve and want themselves. All children want a loving, healthy, and safe environment to grow up in. Helping children be a part of their own pet's care or allowing them to play a role in helping unwanted pets teaches responsibility and accountability in all aspects of life.

Live Like a Dog LLC is an educational company founded by Tracy Voss in 2021. It promotes compassion for all living creatures by publishing books about real rescue dogs and educating children through the PAWS program

Edward's Happy Ending

Edward was rescued from the Brownsville Shelter in October of 2020 and came with a glowing recommendation from the staff. They told us how friendly he was and how much he loved people. He was just "unique."

Edward's face would light up when kids would come to Oliver's House for a visit. He loved them and they loved him. Every time they visited, they wanted to see Edward and his toes. I realized he had another purpose and wasn't ready to leave Oliver's House until I made the decision to crown him The Ambassador for the Live Like a Dog PAWS program. Within days of making this decision, the application came in to adopt him.

He stayed at Tracy's Paws Rescue until July 2021 when he was adopted by Virginia Gibson and her partner David. Edward immediately formed a bond with their dog Little Bit and the two have become inseparable. He has put his street days behind him and can often be found snoozing on the couch or lounging outside in the Texas sun. He loves attention and never passes up a scratch on the head.

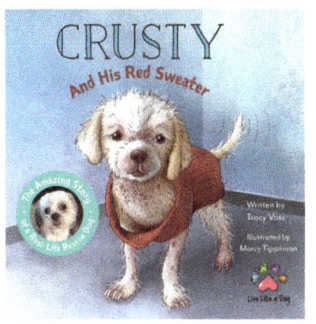

Crusty and His Red Sweater

The Amazing Story of a Real-Life Rescue Dog

This is the true story of how one dog was saved from a life on the streets near the border of Mexico, brought back to health with love and care, and found the perfect home 1,200 miles away from where he started.

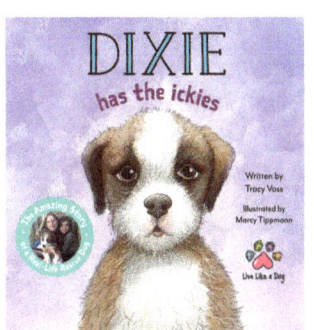

Dixie Has the Ickies

The Amazing Story of a Real-Life Rescue Dog

Little Dixie was born under a porch at a tire shop, where her mom and siblings had too little food and too many bugs. Her luck changed when she was rescued by Dr. Elizabeth, whose friend Tracy worked to find her a wonderful home with an amazing little girl. This is the heartwarming story about a little dog who—despite the rough start to her life—ends up in the best home with a very special purpose.

www.ingramcontent.com/pod-product-compliance
Lightning Source LLC
Chambersburg PA
CBHW051306110526
44589CB00025B/2956